ANIMALS On the Move!

Animals That DIG

by Pearl Markovics

Consultant:
Beth Gambro
Reading Specialist
Yorkville, Illinois

Contents

BEARPORT PUBLISHING

New York, New York

Animals That Dig

What can dig?

A dog can dig.

What can dig?

A pig can dig.

What can dig?

A skunk can dig.

What can dig?

A bear can dig.

What can dig?

A mole can dig.

What can dig?

A squirrel can dig.

Can you dig?

Yes, you can!

Key Words

bear

dog

mole

pig

skunk

squirrel

Index

About the Author

Pearl Markovics loves digging
in the dirt, because she never knows
what she'll find.

Teaching Tips

Before Reading

- ✔ Guide readers on a "picture walk" through the text by asking them to name the animals shown.
- ✔ Discuss book structure by showing children where text will appear consistently on pages.
- ✔ Highlight the supportive pattern, such as the question-and-answer format of the book. Note the consistent number of words found on each alternating page.

During Reading

- ✔ Encourage readers to "read with your finger" and point to each word as it is read. Stop periodically to ask children to point to a specific word in the text.
- ✔ Reading strategies: When encountering unknown words, prompt readers with encouraging cues such as:
    - **Does that word look like a word you already know?**
    - **It could be _____ , but look at _____ .**
    - **Check the picture.**

After Reading

- ✔ Write the key words on index cards.
    - **Have readers match them to pictures in the book.**
    - **Have children sort words by category (words that start with *s*, for example, or are three letters long).**
- ✔ Encourage readers to talk about other animals that dig. Discuss different ways that animals move.
- ✔ Ask readers to identify their favorite page in the book. Have them read that page aloud.

Credits: Cover, © delectus/iStock; 1, © Africa Studio/Shutterstock; 2–3, © Javier Brosch/Shutterstock; 4–5, © Wayne Hutchinson/Alamy; 6–7, © L. Lee Rue/FLPA/Minden Pictures; 8–9, © Ingo Arndt/Alamy; 10–11, © David Cole/Alamy; 12–13, © Andrew Bailey/FLPA/Minden Pictures; 14–15, © matka_Wariatka/Shutterstock; 16T (L to R), © Javier Brosch/Shutterstock, © Richard Mittleman/Gon2Foto/Alamy, and © David Cole/Alamy; 16B (L to R), © Wayne Hutchinson/Alamy, © L. Lee Rue/FLPA/Minden Pictures, and © Andrew Bailey/FLPA/Minden Pictures.

Publisher: Kenn Goin **Senior Editor:** Joyce Tavolacci **Creative Director:** Spencer Brinker

Library of Congress Cataloging-in-Publication Data: Names: Markovics, Pearl, author. Title: Animals that dig / by Pearl Markovics. Description: New York, New York : Bearport Publishing, [2019] | Series: Animals on the move! | Includes bibliographical references and index. Identifiers: LCCN 2018014540 (print) | LCCN 2018020340 (ebook) | ISBN 9781642800296 (Ebook) | ISBN 9781642800074 (library) | ISBN 9781642801422 (pbk.) Subjects: LCSH: Burrowing animals—Juvenile literature. | Animal locomotion—Juvenile literature. Classification: LCC QL756.15 (ebook) | LCC QL756.15 .M325 2019 (print) | DDC 591.56/48–dc23 LC record available at https://lccn.loc.gov/2018014540